HIP-HOP MUSIC

SONGS THAT CHANGED THE WORLD

CROWN SHEPHERD
CICELY LEWIS, EXECUTIVE EDITOR

Lerner Publications ◆ Minneapolis

LETTER FROM CICELY LEWIS

Dear Reader,

Hip-hop has been a part of my life from an early age. I remember using my brush as a microphone and rapping along with Salt-N-Pepa. Hip-hop influenced my fashion, way of speaking, and lifestyle. As a teacher, I shared Tupac's writings to teach poetry elements and Queen Latifah's "U.N.I.T.Y." to help my students better understand the works of poet Maya Angelou.

Cicely Lewis

As a librarian, I want to expose my students to literature that empowers them to take action and that amplifies voices of underrepresented groups. That is what hip-hop does. Hip-hop is more than beats and rhymes; it's a cultural force. For Black people, it's been a spotlight on social justice, and a canvas for our frustrations, joys, and creativity.

As you read the series, think about the power of hip-hop and how it all began. You've probably heard of Cardi B and Nicki Minaj, but who paved the way for them? Reflect on how this musical genre that began in the Black Community is now present around the world.

—Cicely Lewis, Executive Editor

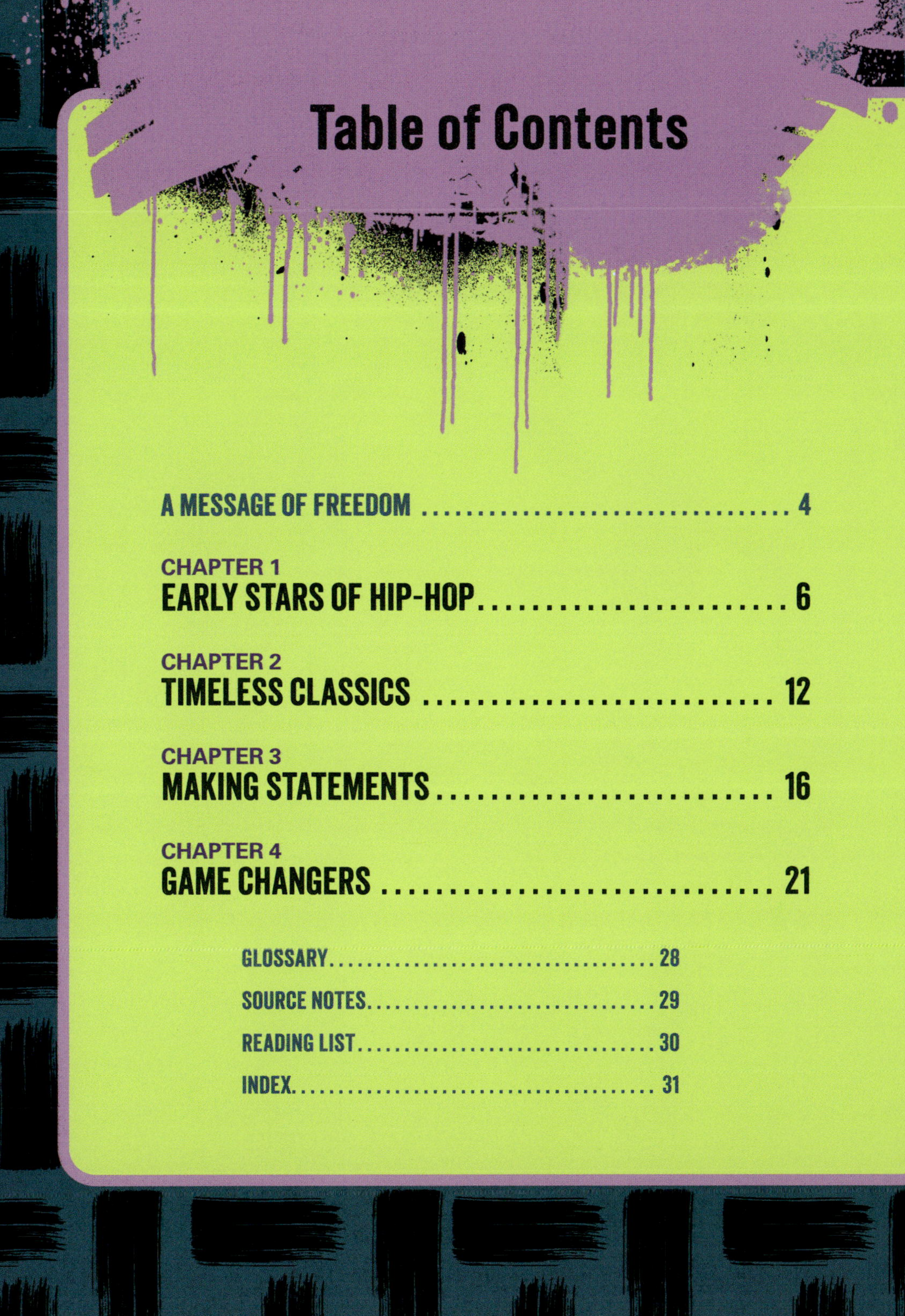

Table of Contents

A MESSAGE OF FREEDOM 4

CHAPTER 1
EARLY STARS OF HIP-HOP 6

CHAPTER 2
TIMELESS CLASSICS 12

CHAPTER 3
MAKING STATEMENTS 16

CHAPTER 4
GAME CHANGERS 21

GLOSSARY 28
SOURCE NOTES 29
READING LIST 30
INDEX 31

A MESSAGE OF FREEDOM

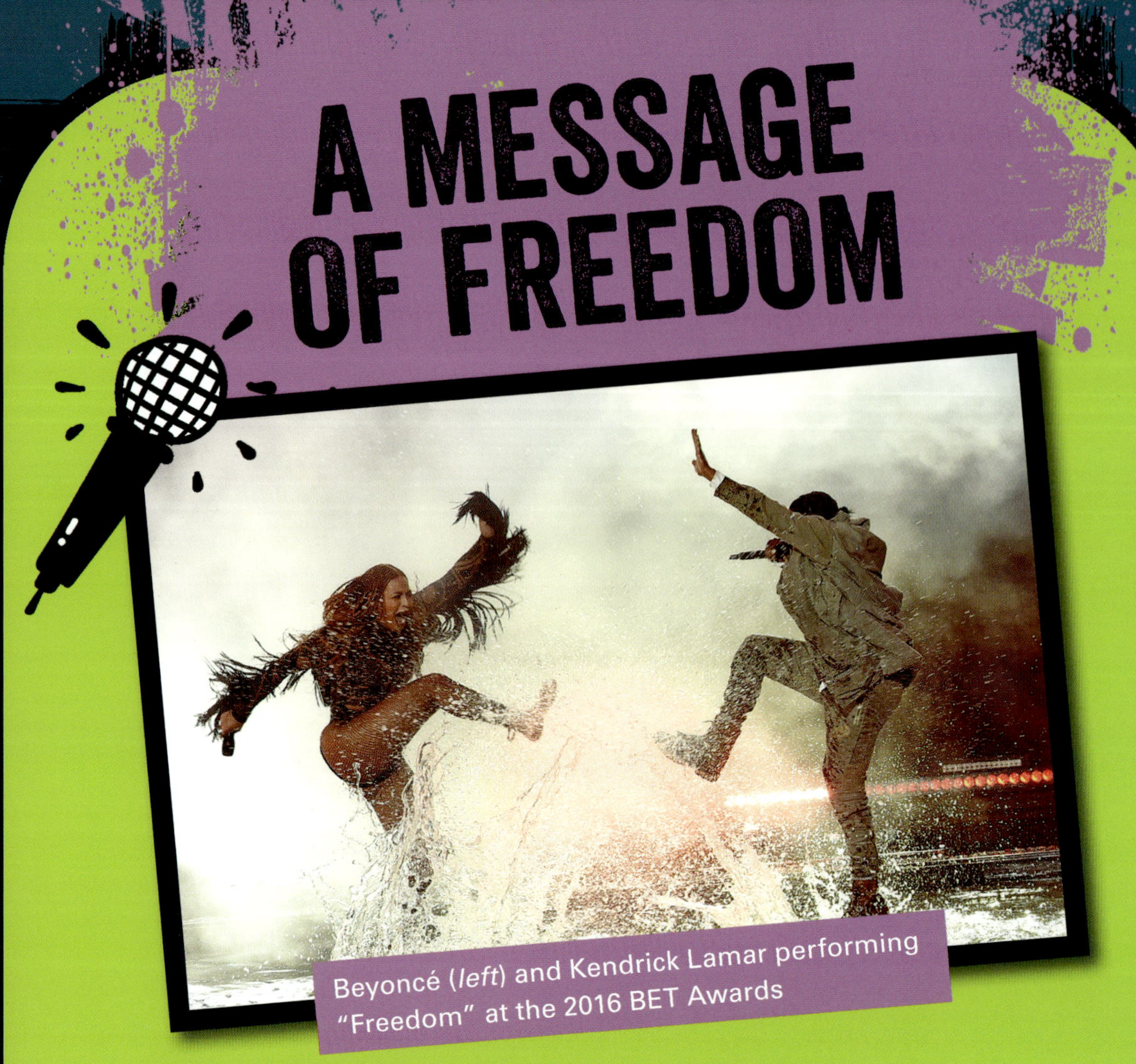

Beyoncé (*left*) and Kendrick Lamar performing "Freedom" at the 2016 BET Awards

EVERY YEAR MILLIONS OF PEOPLE WATCH THE BLACK ENTERTAINMENT TELEVISION (BET) AWARDS, WHICH CELEBRATE THE ACHIEVEMENTS OF BLACK AMERICANS IN MUSIC, SPORTS, TV, AND MOVIES. At the 2016 BET Awards, the audience roared as Beyoncé opened the show with her song "Freedom." A few minutes into the performance, Kendrick Lamar—who is featured on the song—joined Beyoncé onstage.

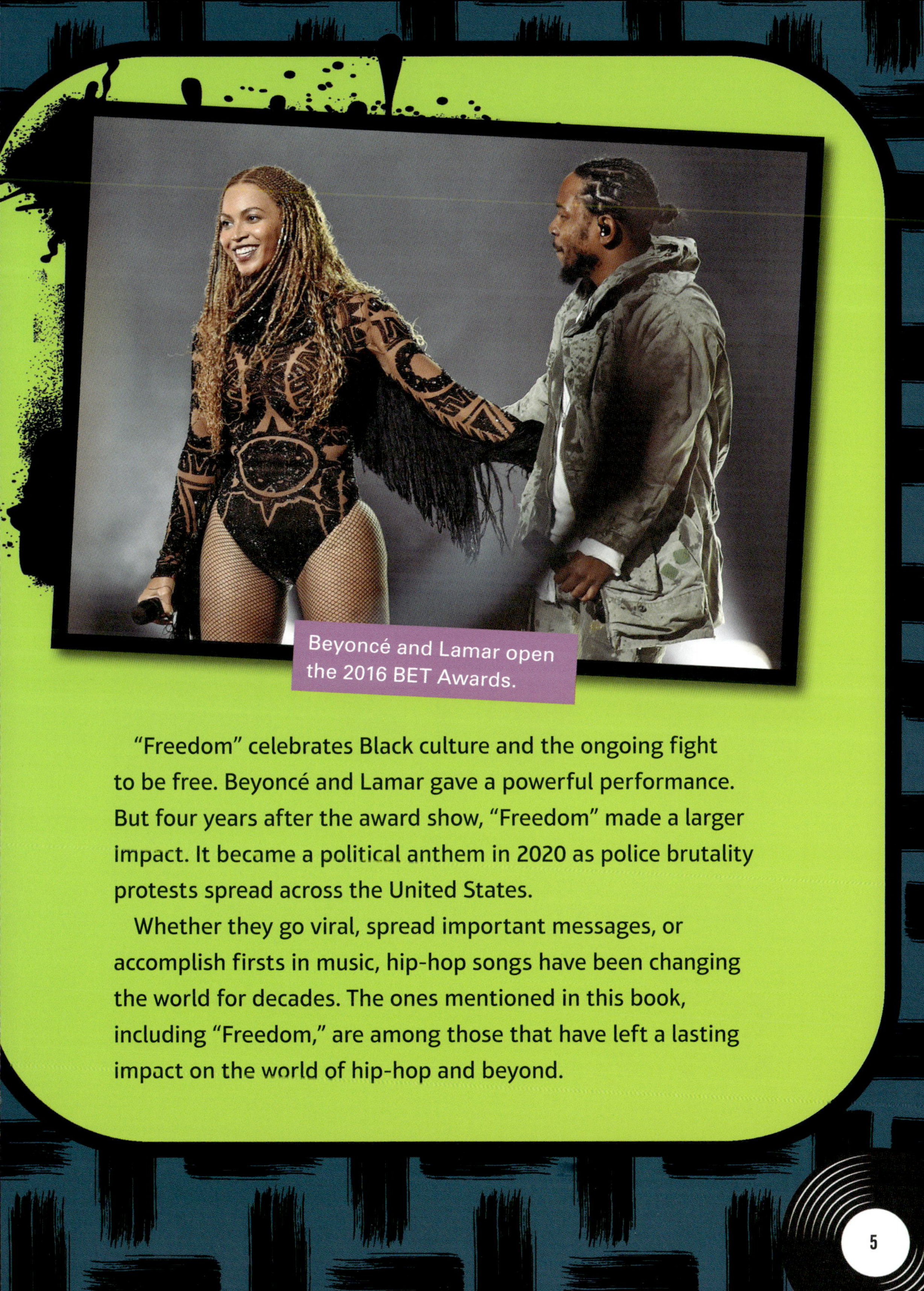

Beyoncé and Lamar open the 2016 BET Awards.

"Freedom" celebrates Black culture and the ongoing fight to be free. Beyoncé and Lamar gave a powerful performance. But four years after the award show, "Freedom" made a larger impact. It became a political anthem in 2020 as police brutality protests spread across the United States.

Whether they go viral, spread important messages, or accomplish firsts in music, hip-hop songs have been changing the world for decades. The ones mentioned in this book, including "Freedom," are among those that have left a lasting impact on the world of hip-hop and beyond.

CHAPTER 1

EARLY STARS OF HIP-HOP

Left to right: Guy "Master Gee" O'Brian, Henry "Big Bank Hank" Jackson, and Michael "Wonder Mike" Wright, the members of The Sugarhill Gang, in 1980

SINCE IT BEGAN IN THE 1970S, HIP-HOP HAS BEEN A MAJOR FORCE IN MUSIC AND CULTURE. Many hip-hop artists and songs have broken barriers and paved the way for other hip-hop artists.

ON THE RADIO

The Sugarhill Gang released their first song, "Rapper's Delight," in 1979. It became the first hip-hop song to play on the radio.

"Rapper's Delight" reached number 36 on *Billboard* Hot 100, which charts the week's most popular songs from all genres. It was the first hip-hop hit to be on the chart, and it was on the chart for twelve weeks. The song spread the hip-hop genre to a wide audience.

The Grammy Hall of Fame was created to honor songs for their lasting impact. In 2014 "Rapper's Delight" joined the Grammy Hall of Fame.

Kurtis Blow performs at Madison Square Garden in 1980.

GOING GOLD

In 1980 Kurtis Blow released his popular song "The Breaks." The song was over seven minutes long and included sounds of funk and disco.

Breakdancers performing in the Bronx in 1984

The song talks about life's hardships, the bad breaks, and life's happy moments, or good breaks. It became popular with young people, especially New York breakdancers. Breakdancing, or breaking, is a type of dance that Black and Latinx youth of the Bronx in New York City created in the 1970s.

"The Breaks" became the first hip-hop song to get gold record status. A gold record is a song or album that has sold five hundred thousand copies.

DJ Jazzy Jeff, or Jeff Townes (*left*), and the Fresh Prince, or Will Smith, win the MTV Award for Best Rap Video in 1989.

FIRST GRAMMY WINNER

The 1988 song "Parents Just Don't Understand" is a song for misunderstood teenagers. It was on the *Billboard* Hot 100 chart for nineteen weeks.

The Grammy Awards are held every year to honor artists for achievements in music. In 1989 DJ Jazzy Jeff & the Fresh Prince won the Grammy for Best Rap Performance, making "Parents Just Don't Understand" the first hip-hop song to win a Grammy. But the hip-hop duo boycotted the Grammy Awards because

DJ Jazzy Jeff (*right*) and the Fresh Prince (*center*) with Ready Rock C, or Clarence Holmes, in 1988

their award category would not be aired on live TV. The song went on to be featured in movies and on the hit show *The Fresh Prince of Bel-Air*, reaching new generations of viewers and listeners.

REFLECT

Do you think it is important that all categories of the Grammy Awards be aired on live TV? Why or why not?

WOMEN'S ANTHEM

Salt-N-Pepa released "None of Your Business" in 1993. Two years later, Salt-N-Pepa won the Grammy award for Best Rap Performance by a Duo or Group. "None of Your Business" was the first hip-hop song by a female group to win in the category.

Left to right: Cheryl "Salt" James, Sandra "Pepa" Denton, and Deidra "DJ Spinderella" Roper, the members of Salt-N-Pepa, win a Grammy award in 1995.

CHAPTER 2

TIMELESS CLASSICS

LL Cool J celebrates winning a Grammy award in 1992.

MUSIC HAS ALWAYS BEEN SHARED THROUGHOUT GENERATIONS. Hip-hop is no different. Songs have the power to remain popular decades after being released.

COMEBACK SONG

By 1990 music critics—people whose job it is to judge or evaluate songs—were saying that LL Cool J was not as strong of a rapper as he was earlier in his career. LL Cool J responded by releasing "Mama Said Knock You Out." The song encourages listeners to believe in themselves and never listen to the haters.

LL Cool J won the Best Rap Solo Performance Grammy award for the song in 1992. "Mama Said Knock You Out" grew in popularity over the years. It sold over two million copies to become a multiplatinum record.

"The song 'Mama Said Knock You Out' didn't get a lot of attention back then. It got a little play on MTV and a little play on radio, but it actually grew over the years. It was strong, but over the years it became a bigger song. That's the craziest thing, and I'm really grateful for that."

—LL Cool J, 2020

SONG OF SELF-LOVE

Lauryn Hill sparked a conversation about self-respect, self-worth, and self-love within relationships when she released her song "Doo Wop (That Thing)" in 1998. The song combines R&B, hip-hop, and soul. Critics described the song as ahead of its time.

"Doo Wop (That Thing)" became the first hip-hop song by a solo woman rapper to hit number 1 on the *Billboard* Hot 100 chart. It was on the chart for twenty-one weeks. Then, in 1999, Hill's song won two Grammys: Best Rhythm & Blues Song and Best Female R&B Vocal Performance.

Lauryn Hill performs at the 1998 *Billboard* Music Awards.

YOUNG DREAMS

Released in 2002, "I Can" by Nas spent twenty weeks on *Billboard* Hot 100, reaching as high as number 12 on the chart. The song tells the youth of the world to believe they can achieve anything they put their minds to. It also talks about the importance of education to achieve these dreams.

"I Can" has been used in school activities to help teach students to be the best versions of themselves. The song is also often used at graduation ceremonies, reaching new audiences over time.

Nas putting on a performance at the 2002 MTV Video Music Awards

REFLECT

Which songs have had the most impact on your life? What about the songs stands out to you?

CHAPTER 3

MAKING STATEMENTS

Rappers (*back row*) DJ Yella, Ice Cube, Chuck D, Eazy-E, Dr. Dre, MC Ren, (*front row*) DJ Train, Laylaw, and The D.O.C. on tour in 1989

SOME SONGS CAN MAKE YOU THINK DIFFERENTLY ABOUT THE WORLD. Whether they address important topics, celebrate diversity, or speak for change, hip-hop artists use their songs to inspire action.

STAND UP

In 1989 actor and director Spike Lee released a movie about racism and violence in a neighborhood of New York City. "Fight the Power" by Public Enemy played throughout the film. The song had a powerful message for its listeners. It told them to stand together and speak up about racism and inequality.

"Fight the Power" reminded people that they have a voice and that their voice has power. It was nominated for Best Rap Performance at the Grammy Awards in 1990. In 2018 "Fight the Power" joined the Grammy Hall of Fame.

Public Enemy attending the 1989 American Music Awards

REFLECT

Hip-hop songs often address social issues such as racism. What are some social issues you care about?

RESPECT FOR WOMEN

Tupac Shakur used his 1993 song "Keep Ya Head Up" to speak for change for women, especially Black women in America. The song talks about treating women with respect, standing up for what's right, and believing in yourself. The song spent twenty weeks on the *Billboard* Hot 100 chart.

Tupac Shakur performs in New York City in 1993.

EQUAL LOVE FOR ALL

"Same Love" by Macklemore & Ryan Lewis and featuring Mary Lambert encourages listeners to love who they want to love no matter what their gender is. Macklemore wrote the song to show his support of his gay family members.

The song challenged the hip-hop world to be more supportive of the LGBTQIA+ community and was used as an anthem during the 2012 fight to legalize same-sex marriage in Washington state. "Same Love" was on the *Billboard* Hot 100 chart for thirty weeks. It was nominated for Song of the Year at the Grammy Awards in 2014.

Mary Lambert (*left*), Macklemore (*center*), and Ryan Lewis win an award for their song "Same Love" at the 2013 MTV Video Music Awards.

"I just wanted to hold myself accountable and hold hip-hop accountable and bring up an issue that was being pushed under the rug."

—Macklemore, 2013

AN IMPORTANT MESSAGE

"DNA." by Kendrick Lamar is about exploring Black culture and celebrating heritage. The 2017 song has inspired listeners with its message. The song sparked conversations about racism, inequality, and violence in America.

Kendrick Lamar performing at the 2017 MTV Video Music Awards

CHAPTER 4

GAME CHANGERS

Missy Elliott in 1998

HIP-HOP IS ALWAYS EVOLVING. By trying new things, artists can change the culture of hip-hop.

Missy Elliott puts on a performance in New York in 1998.

BEST MUSIC VIDEO

Missy Elliott's 1997 song "The Rain (Supa Dupa Fly)" was a celebration of self-expression. In 1998 Elliott was nominated for the Best Rap Solo Performance Grammy award.

"[Supa Dupa Fly] allowed me to work with a lot of different artists and the thing was, they appreciated the fresh new sound that hadn't been heard."

—Missy Elliott, 2022

In the song, Elliott raps about being confident, cool, and unique. She used her music video to show these traits. The music video was colorful, futuristic, and different from what most hip-hop artists were doing at the time. In a 2023 article, *Rolling Stone* magazine named Elliott's music video the best hip-hop video of all time.

REFLECT

The fiftieth anniversary of hip-hop was in 2023. How do you think hip-hop has impacted the world around you? How does early hip-hop influence current artists and other genres of music?

Eminem performs at the 2002 MTV Europe Music Awards in Barcelona, Spain.

MAJOR AWARD WINNER

In 2002 Eminem's song "Lose Yourself" was featured in a movie based on his life. The song talks about facing challenges head-on and never giving up on your dreams. It spent twenty-four weeks on *Billboard* Hot 100 and was number 1 for half of those weeks.

In 2003 Eminem won the Oscar for Best Original Song, making "Lose Yourself" the first hip-hop song to ever win an Oscar. At the Grammy Awards the following year, "Lose Yourself" won Best Rap Song and Best Male Rap Solo Performance.

GOING VIRAL

Soulja Boy's 2007 song "Crank That (Soulja Boy)" spent seven weeks at number 1 on the *Billboard* Hot 100 chart and became a viral dance. By January 2008, it became the first song to have over three million downloads. As of 2024, the music video had over 580 million views on YouTube.

Soulja Boy (*center*) performing at the 2007 BET Hip Hop Awards

Lil Nas X sings his song "Old Town Road" in 2019.

COUNTRY HIP-HOP

Lil Nas X released the country and hip-hop song "Old Town Road" in 2018. The song quickly rose to the top of the *Billboard* Hot Country Songs chart. But shortly after, *Billboard* removed "Old Town Road" from the country list. They said the song did not have enough country elements.

In 2019 Lil Nas X recorded a new version of the song with country singer Billy Ray Cyrus. *Billboard*'s treatment of the song sparked conversations around race and music, especially Black country artists.

In 2021 "Old Town Road" sold fourteen million copies. It became the highest-certified song ever by going platinum fourteen times.

Lil Nas X celebrates winning Grammy awards in 2020.

ONGOING MUSIC

For over fifty years, hip-hop songs have influenced the world. The songs have driven activism and shed light on important social issues. This genre of music continues to grow, and new award-winning artists will keep sparking change.

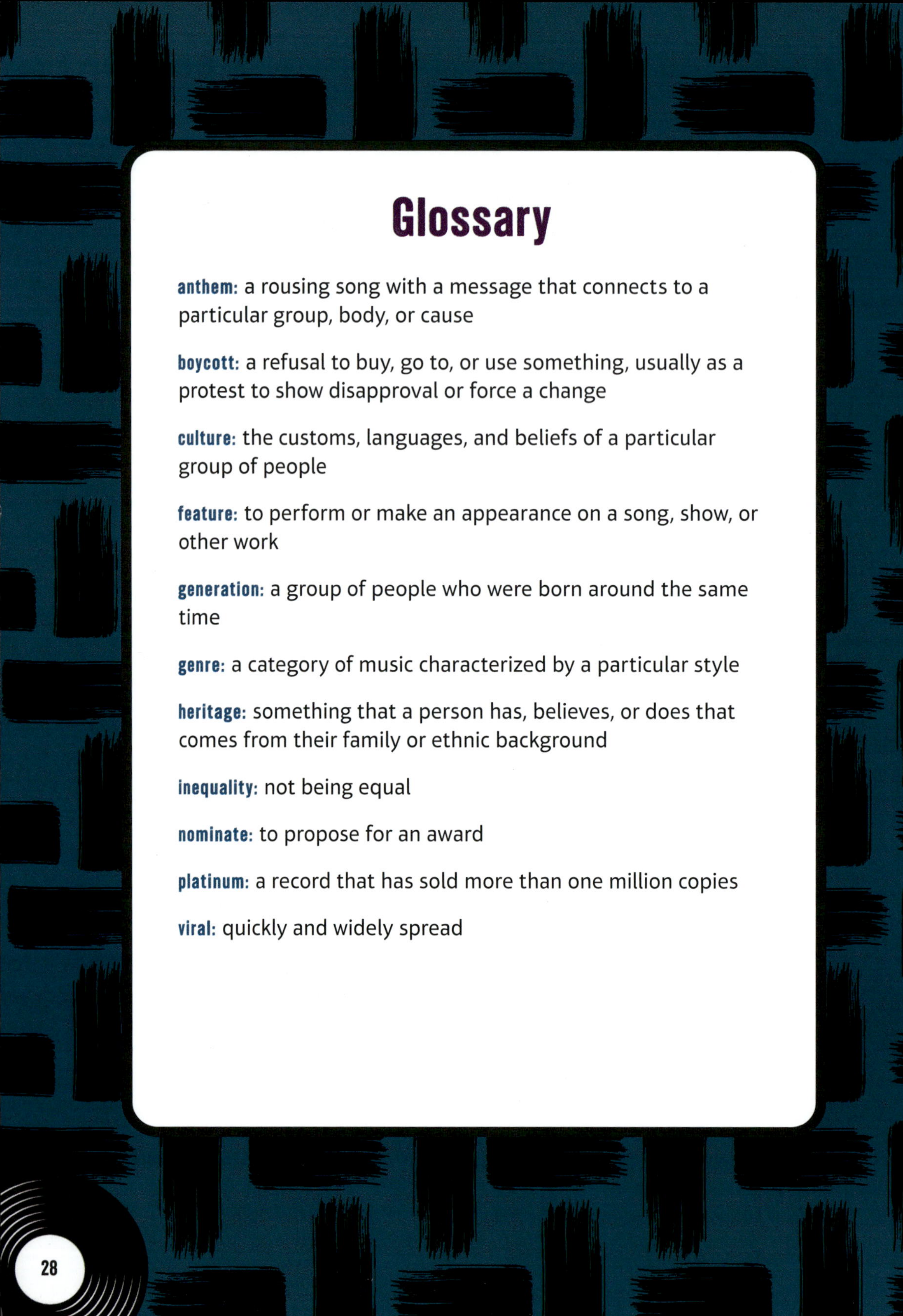

Glossary

anthem: a rousing song with a message that connects to a particular group, body, or cause

boycott: a refusal to buy, go to, or use something, usually as a protest to show disapproval or force a change

culture: the customs, languages, and beliefs of a particular group of people

feature: to perform or make an appearance on a song, show, or other work

generation: a group of people who were born around the same time

genre: a category of music characterized by a particular style

heritage: something that a person has, believes, or does that comes from their family or ethnic background

inequality: not being equal

nominate: to propose for an award

platinum: a record that has sold more than one million copies

viral: quickly and widely spread

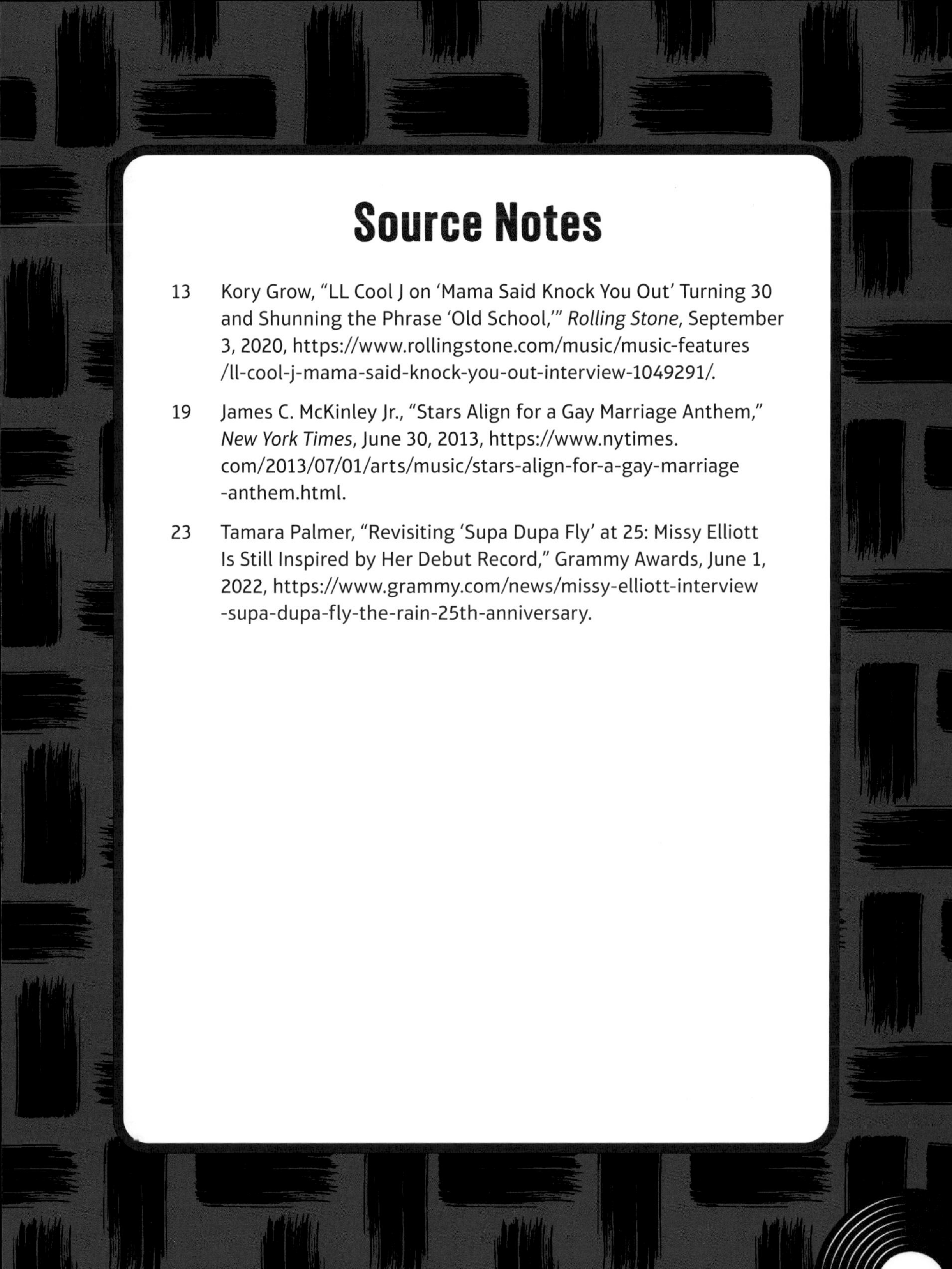

Source Notes

13 Kory Grow, "LL Cool J on 'Mama Said Knock You Out' Turning 30 and Shunning the Phrase 'Old School,'" *Rolling Stone*, September 3, 2020, https://www.rollingstone.com/music/music-features/ll-cool-j-mama-said-knock-you-out-interview-1049291/.

19 James C. McKinley Jr., "Stars Align for a Gay Marriage Anthem," *New York Times*, June 30, 2013, https://www.nytimes.com/2013/07/01/arts/music/stars-align-for-a-gay-marriage-anthem.html.

23 Tamara Palmer, "Revisiting 'Supa Dupa Fly' at 25: Missy Elliott Is Still Inspired by Her Debut Record," Grammy Awards, June 1, 2022, https://www.grammy.com/news/missy-elliott-interview-supa-dupa-fly-the-rain-25th-anniversary.

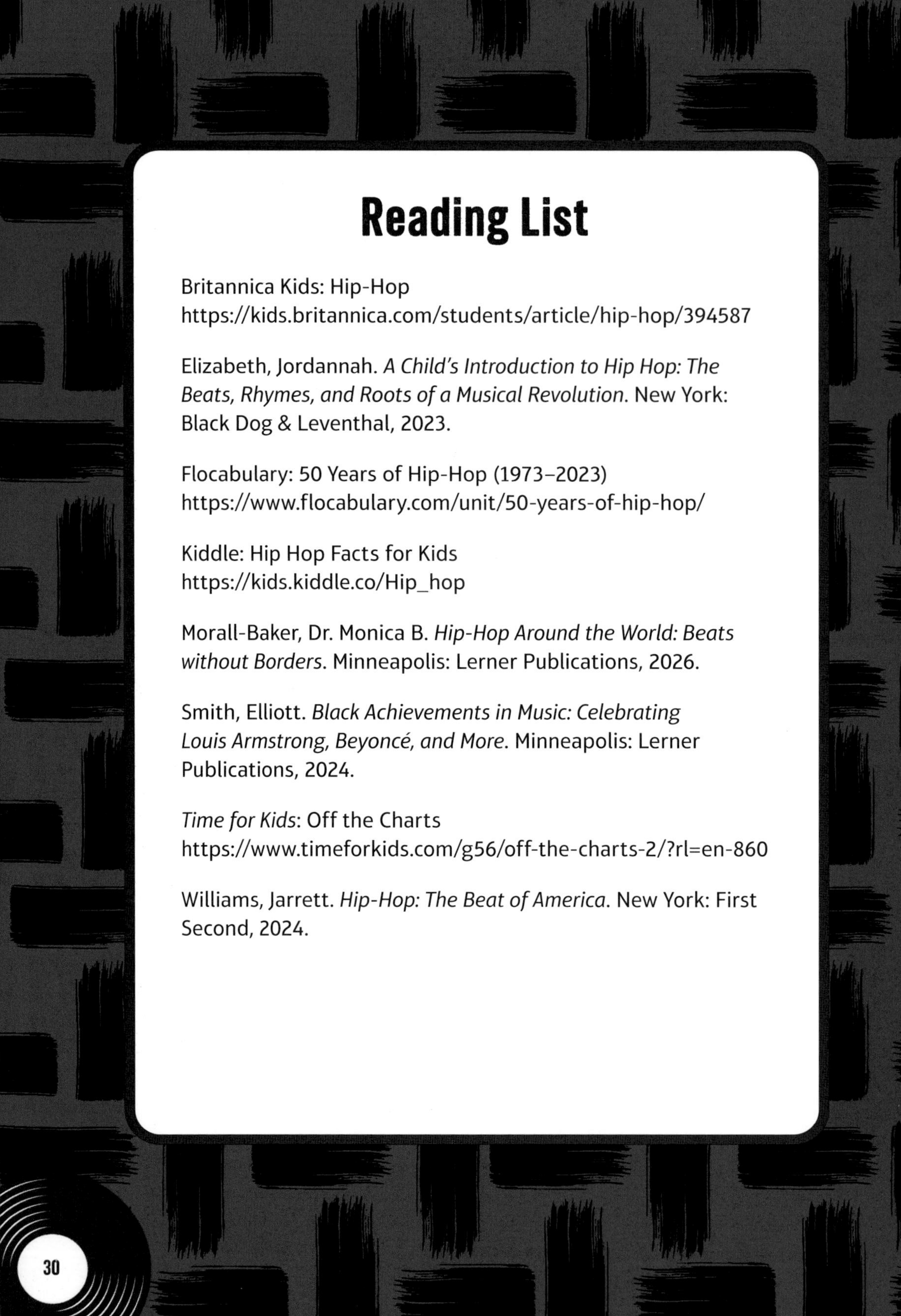

Reading List

Britannica Kids: Hip-Hop
https://kids.britannica.com/students/article/hip-hop/394587

Elizabeth, Jordannah. *A Child's Introduction to Hip Hop: The Beats, Rhymes, and Roots of a Musical Revolution*. New York: Black Dog & Leventhal, 2023.

Flocabulary: 50 Years of Hip-Hop (1973–2023)
https://www.flocabulary.com/unit/50-years-of-hip-hop/

Kiddle: Hip Hop Facts for Kids
https://kids.kiddle.co/Hip_hop

Morall-Baker, Dr. Monica B. *Hip-Hop Around the World: Beats without Borders*. Minneapolis: Lerner Publications, 2026.

Smith, Elliott. *Black Achievements in Music: Celebrating Louis Armstrong, Beyoncé, and More*. Minneapolis: Lerner Publications, 2024.

Time for Kids: Off the Charts
https://www.timeforkids.com/g56/off-the-charts-2/?rl=en-860

Williams, Jarrett. *Hip-Hop: The Beat of America*. New York: First Second, 2024.

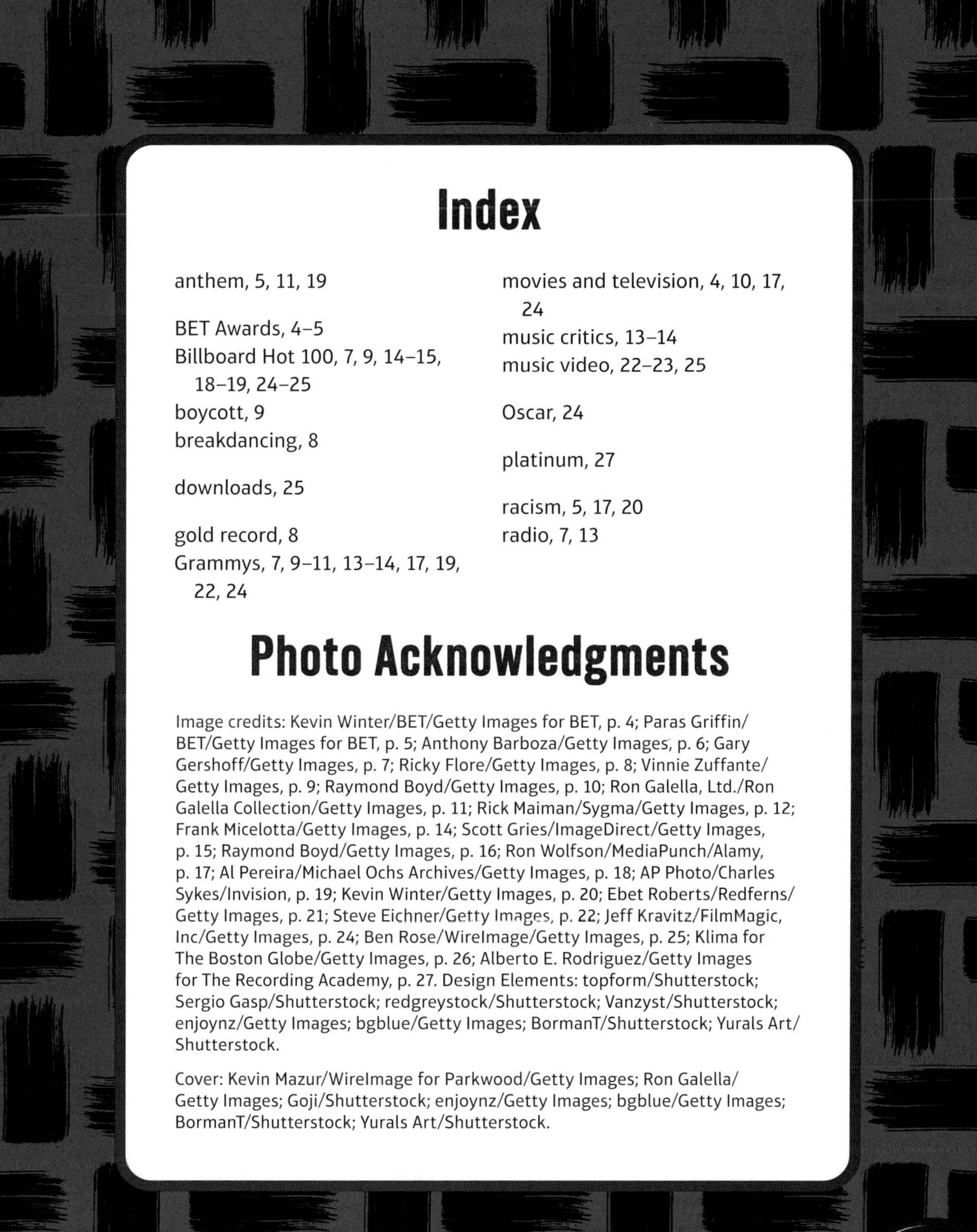

Index

anthem, 5, 11, 19

BET Awards, 4–5
Billboard Hot 100, 7, 9, 14–15, 18–19, 24–25
boycott, 9
breakdancing, 8

downloads, 25

gold record, 8
Grammys, 7, 9–11, 13–14, 17, 19, 22, 24

movies and television, 4, 10, 17, 24
music critics, 13–14
music video, 22–23, 25

Oscar, 24

platinum, 27

racism, 5, 17, 20
radio, 7, 13

Photo Acknowledgments

Image credits: Kevin Winter/BET/Getty Images for BET, p. 4; Paras Griffin/BET/Getty Images for BET, p. 5; Anthony Barboza/Getty Images, p. 6; Gary Gershoff/Getty Images, p. 7; Ricky Flore/Getty Images, p. 8; Vinnie Zuffante/Getty Images, p. 9; Raymond Boyd/Getty Images, p. 10; Ron Galella, Ltd./Ron Galella Collection/Getty Images, p. 11; Rick Maiman/Sygma/Getty Images, p. 12; Frank Micelotta/Getty Images, p. 14; Scott Gries/ImageDirect/Getty Images, p. 15; Raymond Boyd/Getty Images, p. 16; Ron Wolfson/MediaPunch/Alamy, p. 17; Al Pereira/Michael Ochs Archives/Getty Images, p. 18; AP Photo/Charles Sykes/Invision, p. 19; Kevin Winter/Getty Images, p. 20; Ebet Roberts/Redferns/Getty Images, p. 21; Steve Eichner/Getty Images, p. 22; Jeff Kravitz/FilmMagic, Inc/Getty Images, p. 24; Ben Rose/WireImage/Getty Images, p. 25; Klima for The Boston Globe/Getty Images, p. 26; Alberto E. Rodriguez/Getty Images for The Recording Academy, p. 27. Design Elements: topform/Shutterstock; Sergio Gasp/Shutterstock; redgreystock/Shutterstock; Vanzyst/Shutterstock; enjoynz/Getty Images; bgblue/Getty Images; BormanT/Shutterstock; Yurals Art/Shutterstock.

Cover: Kevin Mazur/WireImage for Parkwood/Getty Images; Ron Galella/Getty Images; Goji/Shutterstock; enjoynz/Getty Images; bgblue/Getty Images; BormanT/Shutterstock; Yurals Art/Shutterstock.

To all the individuals who are using art to make a difference in the world

Lerner Publications Company
An imprint of Lerner Publishing Group, Inc.
241 First Avenue North
Minneapolis, MN 55401 USA

For reading levels and more information, look up this title at www.lernerbooks.com.

Main body text set in Aptifer Sans LT Pro.
Typeface provided by Linotype AG.

Library of Congress Cataloging-in-Publication Data

Names: Shepherd, Crown, author.
Title: Hip-hop music : songs that changed the world / Crown Shepherd.
Description: Minneapolis : Lerner Publications, 2026. | Series: Hip-hop culture | Includes bibliographical references and index. | Audience: Ages 9–14 | Audience: Grades 4–6 | Summary: "Whether they won major awards or carried important messages, many hip-hop songs have sparked changes in the world. Learn about important hip-hop songs from artists such as Public Enemy, Missy Elliott, and Kendrick Lamar"— Provided by publisher.
Identifiers: LCCN 2024037172 (print) | LCCN 2024037173 (ebook) | ISBN 9798765659830 (library binding) | ISBN 9798765684269 (paperback) | ISBN 9798765677971 (epub)
Subjects: LCSH: Rap (Music)—History and criticism—Juvenile literature. | Hip-hop—Juvenile literature.
Classification: LCC ML3531 .S465 2025 (print) | LCC ML3531 (ebook) | DDC 782.421649—dc23/eng/20240815

LC record available at https://lccn.loc.gov/2024037172
LC ebook record available at https://lccn.loc.gov/2024037173

Manufactured in the United States of America
1-1011684-53630-10/30/2024